D1359505

# This book belongs to:

Peyton smith ♡♡☆

Edition: 1.0

Find 9 differences between the two pictures.

Find 8 differences between the pictures above.
Find 9 differences between the pictures below.

Find 12 differences between the two pictures.

Find 8 differences between the pictures above.
Find 7 differences between the pictures below.

Find 12 differences between the two pictures.

Find 8 differences between the pictures above.
Find 7 differences between the pictures below.

Find 7 differences between the two pictures.

Find 6 differences between the two pictures.

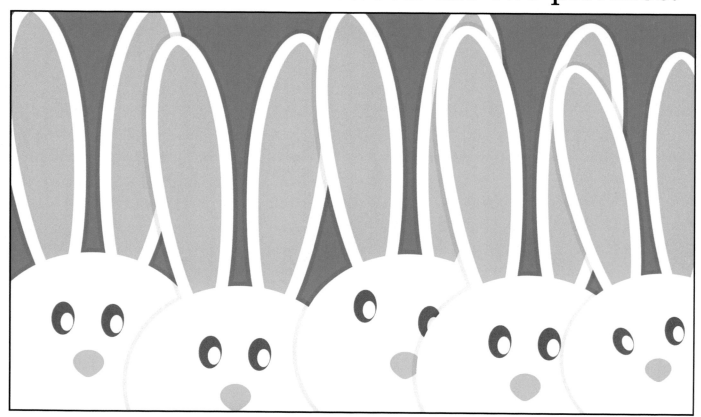

Find 6 differences between the pictures above.
Find 5 differences between the pictures below.

# Find 10 differences between the two pictures.

Find 7 differences between the pictures above.
Find 9 differences between the pictures below.

Find 12 differences between the two pictures.

Find 6 differences between the pictures above.
Find 7 differences between the pictures below.

Find 8 differences between the two pictures.

Find 6 differences between the pictures above.
Find 9 differences between the pictures below.

Find 7 differences between the pictures above.
Find 8 differences between the pictures below.

Find 9 differences between the two pictures.

Find 6 differences between the pictures above.
Find 7 differences between the pictures below.

# Find 10 differences between the two pictures.

Find 9 differences between the two pictures.

Find 8 differences between the pictures above.
Find 7 differences between the pictures below.

Find 8 differences between the two pictures.

Find 12 differences between the pictures above.
Find 10 differences between the pictures below.

Find 7 differences between the pictures above.
Find 8 differences between the pictures below.

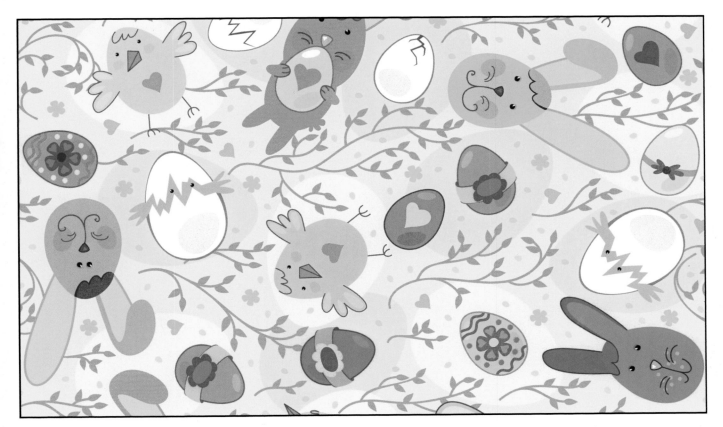

# Find 13 differences between the two pictures.

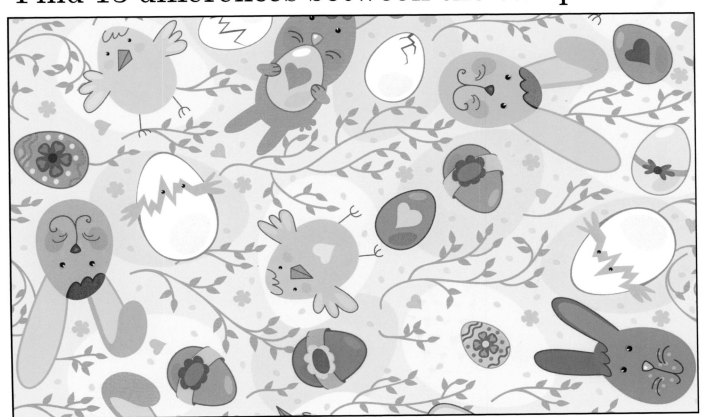

Find 5 differences between the pictures above.
Find 6 differences between the pictures below.

Find 10 differences between the two pictures.

Find 9 differences between the pictures above.
Find 6 differences between the pictures below.

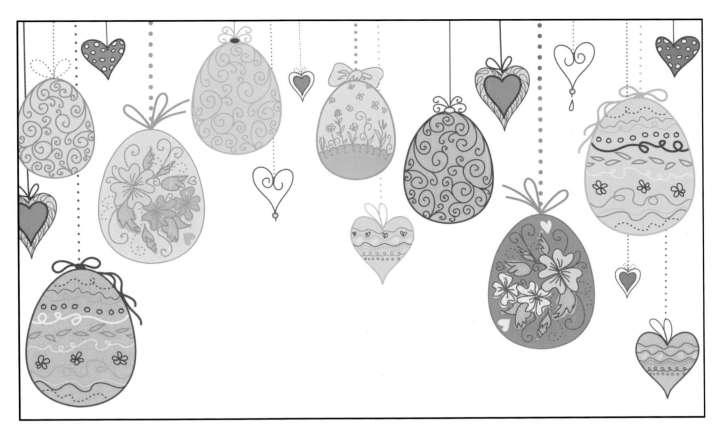

# Find 12 differences between the two pictures.

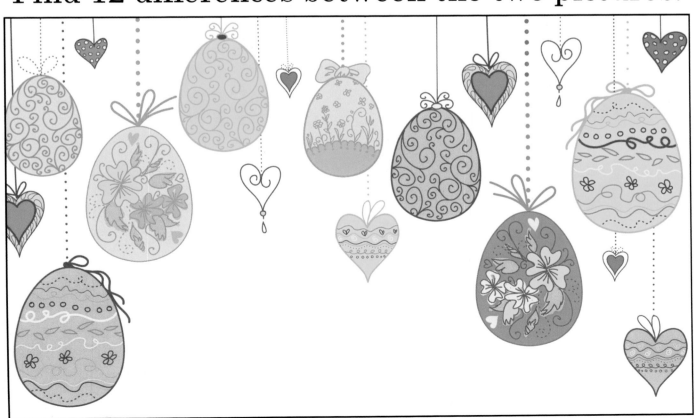

Find 8 differences between the pictures above.
Find 9 differences between the pictures below.

Find 8 differences between the two pictures.

Find 10 differences between the two pictures.

Find 6 differences between the pictures above.
Find 7 differences between the pictures below.

Find 8 differences between the two pictures.

Find 7 differences between the pictures above.
Find 9 differences between the pictures below.

# SPOT THE DIFFERENCES

## Answers

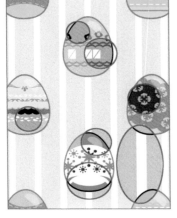

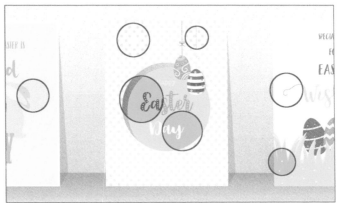
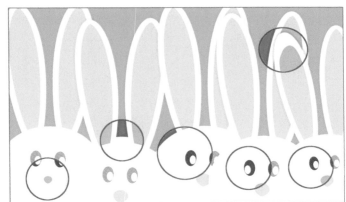

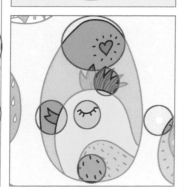

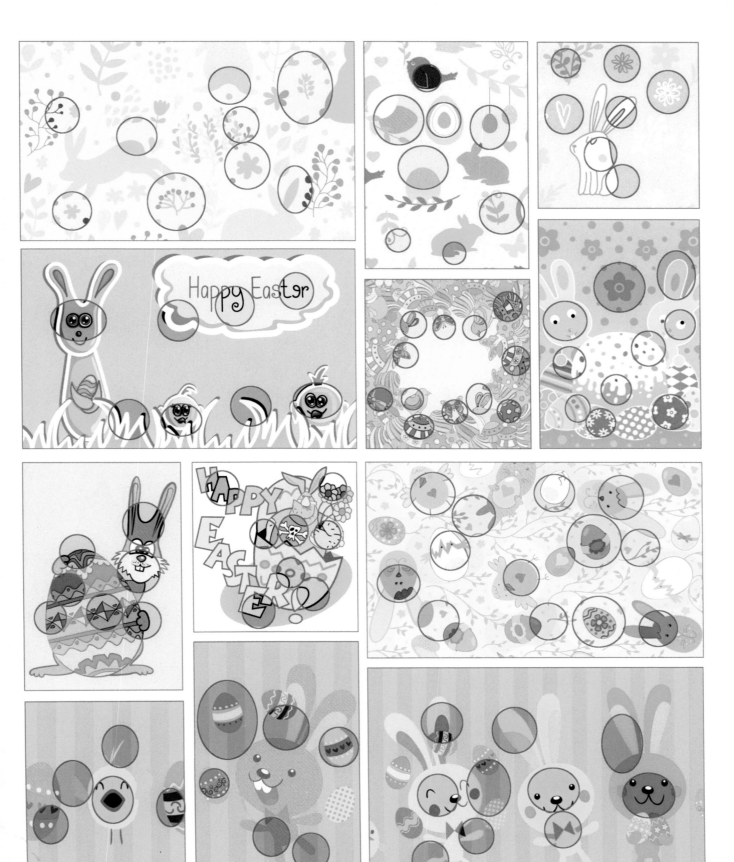

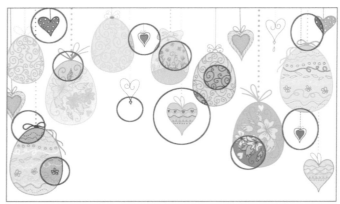

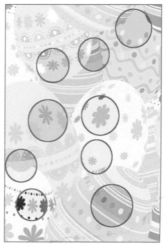

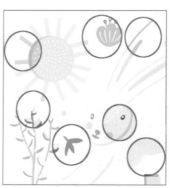